Incompleteness Theory

poems by

Danèlle Lejeune

Finishing Line Press
Georgetown, Kentucky

Incompleteness Theory

Copyright © 2025 by Danèlle Lejeune
ISBN 979-8-89990-039-6 First Edition
All rights reserved under International and Pan-American Copyright Conventions. No part of this book may be reproduced in any manner whatsoever without written permission from the publisher, except in the case of brief quotations embodied in critical articles and reviews.

ACKNOWLEDGMENTS

Concupiscence published by *Olive Press* 2017
Cancer published by *Drunk Monkeys* 2018
Canyons, P = (P.x,P.y,P.c) was published by *Driftwood* press 2018
Calculation published by *Whale Road Review* 2020
Astrophysics of Victimology published by *Gyroscope Review* 2022
Cultivating Spooky Action, Couples Therapy for Bulldozers, True North, Cantor's Set Theory, & Scientists Found Ripples in Space and Time published by *Mud Season Review* 2024
Perseids (as Feu Follet) published by *McNeese Review* 2022

Publisher: Leah Huete de Maines
Editor: Christen Kincaid
Cover Art: A mixed media painting by Danèlle Lejeune
Author Photo: Taylor Christine Hayes and Danèlle Lejeune
Cover Design: Elizabeth Maines McCleavy

Order online: www.finishinglinepress.com
also available on amazon.com

Author inquiries and mail orders:
Finishing Line Press
PO Box 1626
Georgetown, Kentucky 40324
USA

Contents

Scientists Found Ripples in Space and Time 1

Compass: True North 2

Coordinates, (the Purple: God) 3

Concupiscence 4

Zika Corona 5

Eclipse 7

For Frack Sake, Honey—Couples Therapy for Bulldozers 8

Cultivating Spooky Action at a Distance, a Love Letter 9

Einstein Cross 11

Astrophysics of Victimology 12

Constellation 13

The Perseids 14

Cantor's Set Theory 15

Canyons, $P = (P.x, P.y, P.c)$ 16

A diagnosis, a meme 17

Skeleton of a fever of stingrays 18

Cancer: Daily Horoscope for Summer Solstice 19

Calculation: Waiting for Gödel 20

To the love of many lifetimes, forever and ever.
Love, Blue

'The idea that everything in the world has meaning is, by the way, the exact analogue of the principle that everything has a cause on which the whole of science is based.'
—Kurt Gödel in a letter to his Mother in October, 1961

Scientists Found Ripples in Space and Time
And You Have to Buy Groceries

> *We've just learned that the whole universe is humming around us. Now what?*
> —Adam Frank, *The Atlantic*

The grocery list grows and shrinks, pulsating.
This week bananas, apples, tampons,
extra hamburger, and poster board.

There could be more to this.
The night sky is a haze
because we all leave our porch lights on—

waiting for some hero, an astronaut maybe?
Some Orion to unsheathe a blade
and slay the bill collectors

or the horny old men at the gas station—
who drunk-ask me to come home with them:
I respond, *you do not want this liability.*

From my car in that gas station parking lot,
gnats look like shooting stars in the upward haze—
crashing, waiting for wishes and children.

The groceries in the backseat melting,
the stolen gas station toilet paper in my purse.
Lipstick cakes and blisters my bottom lip.

It's not the universe humming, it's the broken
hot water heater that sometimes gets too hot
and other times blows a fuse and smokes.

This week's groceries include extra milk,
crayons, diet coke, a raspberry chocolate bar,
light bulbs, batteries, and bug spray.

Compass: True North
for Mary Jane Oliver (September 10, 1935 – January 17, 2019)

> "Something strange is going on at the top of the world.
> Earth's north magnetic pole has been skittering away."
> —Alexandra Witze

I opened up my heart. "Anemia," the nurse said. "Not eating
enough meat? Bleeding too much, not enough..." No.
"My blood thins *driven by liquid iron sloshing within my core.*"

*The problem lies partly with irrational sadness
and partly with other seismic shifts deep within...*
The nurse writes in my chart and leaves the room.

*The core generates most of the magnetic field,
which changes over time as the deep flows shift.*
So much has changed. Navigation is impossible.

It started with...so many red flags and a poem.
Not a pole. A poem. A cup of coffee. A phone call.
I pulled to astronavigate, but cloud cover is 90%.

I read Mary's *"Wild Geese"* five hundred days in a row.
*In 2019, the poem crossed the International Line and I am
currently making a beeline for Siberia.* So they think. I think

*The fault lines are so inaccurate that cell count exceeds
the acceptable limit for navigational errors
and has shattered my internal compass.*

"Wild Geese" became my compass. Now
the poem has sloshed. Sometimes you have to go
into the frozen tundra to go home. *Do I have to be good?*

This, my magnetic field changed so dramatically.
Because I was tired and lonely and done, and that means
I am essentially losing a magnetic tug-of-war.
My careful braid would have come undone, my blood thinned,
no matter the poem. Maybe. Always. Yes. Oh yes.

Coordinates, (the Purple: God)

My daughter finger painted a landscape of reds, grey, and purple.
She told me it was Mt. Vesuvius: The red part: people dying.
The grey: ash rising and rock smoking. The Purple: God.

There was a bit of yellow because "Yellow flowers made Mama happy
once." We drove across South Dakota barren badlands, she whispered,
Vol—caan—no—noes... her four-year-old word for volcanoes. God

on the horizon, a heat *mama-rage*, painting everything rose
gold. All of Yellowstone will explode someday, maybe sinking
the bears, the sulfur hot springs, too-hot water turned purple

with snowmelt. Were we swimming in salt or salvation?
Happy, I woke in our tent one morning, feeling tremors in the bed-
rock, a sudden absence of birdsong, and the scent of burning

Ponderosa Pine. July snowfall surprised me, bird-sized geometries,
cold and sweet clarity. I wondered if ash would fall like incendiary
book pages, the fire on the mountainside cannot hold back the rising.

Would you find us thousands of years later, posed in purple rock,
mother and daughter curled up together, dreaming of bears?

Concupiscence

Light is made of tiny particles of minutes and seconds,
and little bites of time, bits of glittering pieces
that only move in a straight line with finite velocity, possibility.
Adam says that God exists between these lines:

the human soul is poetry and divine relationship.
The difference: there are only a certain amount of rhymes.
Other poets believe that line breaks are possible, that God
uses the lines to exit stage left, behind a velveteen curtain.

I dream of light, the echoing boom of old voices
down the hallway of my throat and I swallow
the formulas, chalky, dusty between graphite
notes, wood sharp from knife shaved tips.

The corpuscular theory bleeds into porous materials,
the wood floors, worn thin from scraping shoes,
salt tracked in from the icy roads, mudslush melting
and staining the carpet threads with oil and exhaustion.

Each cell speaks of its own pain, attacked alone,
fending off knife wounds and papercuts with multiplication
and odd scraps of paper, found around the house, clotting
between mattress and box spring, inside pillows, dreaming.

Light is made of words, clock hands, man-made fears,
cherry pies, strong coffee. Darkness is the silence
that comes when the particles leave you. I keep looking
for you looking for the exit sign, glowing blue over the door.

I'll never get used to the leaving, the sound of crushed gravel,
the receding headlights in the rain, flickering light.
The universe is tangled around my neck again.
The clasp broke, leaving the asteroids wrapping chains

around Mars and Earth, they collide, the stones chip.

Zika Corona

Humans are   slow
and,

we can't   outrun
anything.

Mosquitoes are   the best
taking us   down.

A small   letting,
a bit of   blood,

drawn shallow
but deliberate.

Welt raising on sandy skin,
the itch an unbearable   crescendo.

Humans are   weak and slow,
we can't   out

think ourselves,
though, we think   we can.

Fall down, forget   time?
Remember we are   still

top of the pile,
meat and bone,

the food chain,   ankle
and Earth   bound,

gravity betraying
our dreams of dry   land.

The moment total darkness,
is night in day,
will I be afraid?

Eclipse

The night we met, I was hungry
and have been full ever since.

Look at how, now, I smile, bellyful
laugh like breaking ocean waves.

Sand between my teeth, and hair,
blood between my toes and fingernails,

I watch the moonrise with your ghost,
shadow-snakes run up the tidal dunes,

after midnight static wobbling
like old tube and knob television,

the memory of fear that came with the white noise
and crackle pop of nothing airing.

Erring. I have made a blinding error. What?
I looked directly at the sun, the moon pretending.

I should have watched the shadows tug and
pull around my feet and tangle, twist, tight.

Now all I see is fire, planets, stars falling.
What's the difference between a meteor and a comet?

One has entered my atmosphere,
the other I watched pull away and leave.

One falls like glitter on the waves, magic—

For Frack Sake, Honey—Couples Therapy for Bulldozers

Previously hidden faults
will fracture when stress
is overcome by the pressure
                      of everything.
Fracturing
at great depth frequently
triggered and suppressed by pressure
due to the weight of the overlying
                      everything.
              Triggering
earthquakes,
along with hazards to public health
and the home environment
                      of everything.
              Along the deepest
fault the big machines
up the hill, strike down pounding over and over
making music, bass beat, and *thunk*,
                      everything.
Up here, sedimentary
beds run nearly
horizontal, made up in twisted sheets,
smoothed corners every morning,
                      everything
dusted clean.

Horizontal and previously unknown
faults rise to the occasion and tenor—
become weapons of economic destruction
                      everything.

            Rising
oil spills wine-dark over soil,
carried by sand and water by striking
hard, over and over, over everything.

Cultivating Spooky Action at a Distance, a Love Letter

The blue rocking chair sometimes
sounds like your boot-fall on porch boards,
a steady pacing, the autumn wind impatient.

A bee lands on my dress sleeve,
tiny cornflowers on white cotton worn thin—
I see nothing but star hungry darkness
and stinger, fractal eyes, and I know

this loneliness is a paradox,
a paradox is that measurement
made when either of the particles

collapses the state of the entanglement
instantaneously, before any coffee can be made,
before any result could have been communicated,

faster than light. We are spinning.
The distance and timing cannot be chosen.
A letter arrives, and then another.
I miss you and yet, you and I are

the interval between the two measurements,
connecting the events, would have to travel 1,200 miles
faster than light, I begin to wonder.

For two spacelike separated events x1 and x2 there are inertial frames
in which x1 is first and others in which x2 is first—
correlation between the two cannot be explained

as one measurement is determining the other:
different observers would disagree about the role of cause and effect.
Different observers like to disagree, loudly, at church picnics.

Entanglement is an area of extreme effects
demonstrated experimentally with small diamonds
worn on the left hand, with delicate reserve.

*If a pair of particles are generated in such a way
that their total spin is known to be zero, and one particle
is found to have clockwise spin on a certain axis, the spin*

*of the other particle, measured on the same axis, will be found
to be counterclockwise, as to be expected,* in June,
due to their entanglement.

*It appears that one particle of an entangled pair knows
what measurement has been performed on the other,
which at the time of measurement may separate—*

by arbitrarily large distances. This distance is not intentional.
This loneliness is a paradox. This blue rocking chair is a time machine. We are rocking. We are spinning.

Einstein Cross

Scientists found the evidence of God
far, far away. Blue nuggets.

Proof of something.

These are galaxies that are interrupted.
Something has changed them, but not enough
to stop them from making more stars,

these hearts of galaxies expand into more stars,

more stars,

more stars.

Yet,

the heart is still incomplete,
unstable, missing elements
and that's what
the satellites are stuck
with—

incomplete images
of beautiful patterns.

Always the same, maybe.
Proof of something.

Astrophysics of Victimology

> *"What is in motion stays in motion.*
> *unless acted upon by an unbalanced force."*
> —Albert Einstein

A statistic says that abused women are uneducated—
Black holes behind an event horizon,
Closed time like curves…what's in motion stays in motion.
Dear reader, IQ and education do not protect women.
Einstein's theory has physical consequences.
Forget what you know about who stays and who goes—
Geodesic motion is part of General Relativity.
Hole. Black hole. Black Whole. Whole. An unbalanced force.
Ignore the electron's angular moments.
Just stop. All of it hurts. All of it hurts.
Kindness of strangers can feel like pity
Like our itchy sweaters, like our names—What if the
Magnetic movement of an object could match our pain, our
Naked singularity? Our space-time? Our light. Our constant.
Our gravity. Sometimes we feel so alone. A singularity.
Planck's constant measures what matters and what is left.
Quantum electrodynamics is how light and matter interact.
Ring singularity does not have a diamond after all.
Schwarzschild radius rs of mass is radius is…the distance from
The center of a non-rotating black hole to the event horizon.
Understand this. Anyone can fall into a black hole.
Victims are not everyone else, not you, not deserving.
Where can you unlearn these theories, in theory? You can
Xerox the fliers, hand them out, hope that 1-800 works.
You may look in a mirror one day and see Schrödinger's cat.
Zero clue how you got here, who you are now, how to leave.

Constellation

A constant stirring of stars:
how I always imagined the glittering
morning dew or early frost
when the whole world sparkles like
a dream, even the brown, melting
gutter slush, even the dented trash cans,
a dead squirrel zapped by the transformer,
icicles hanged for their crimes from the roofline.
I know the frozen daggers are caused by warmth,
the too-hot wood stove, the draughts escaping
like ghosts sliding up the attic stairs.
But here in the doorway between
steaming kitchen and dwindling woodpile,
I breathe out glass shards, spirits,
a constellation of coffee and stale morning breath.
A stellation, a constant.
A dying star.

The Perseids

This trace is what's left of us.
I look for the weight of light, the particles
falling down my breasts like crumbs. The mass
of the universe is choking me, leaving
           lines, chain burns, gouges deep into my chest.

These pieces of you, pieces of me, we
are stardust. The music of gravity hums
between our bodies, the pull betrayed
constellations, set them on fire.
                      They are falling into the sea.

Each burn blisters the mass, the inertia
a measure of resistance my body
offers, an application of force.
                Every August, we watch them die.

Every September, we forget that they lie
at the silted bottom of the sea. Buried in sand,
buried here, burned, and drowned. My body is
           a ghost ship, seaworthy at half sail.

Cantor's Set Theory

{x:x=all the grief, the wailing and moaning, the broken hearts
this set contains me and the number 3.
The number 3=y and y is all of my children.
x + y * the whole of who I am at any given time}

Canyons, P = (P.x,P.y,P.z)

Flesh tensed and burned under my fingertips,
following the curves and lines of laughter.

Benoit Mandelbrot whispered one morning,
"Beautiful, damn hard, increasingly useful. That's fractals."

A never ending pattern, a prison of lines and edges.
How do we become unstuck?

Fractured, a spiral break, deep into bone,
rarely an accident and hard to ignore.

My arm aches sometimes when the morning
is damp and cold, the line of the canyon carved deep.

I dream Benoit lifts my arm and kisses it,
tenderness fades back into the tea steam.

Car doors slamming, gravel dust, blood.
How can the patterns go on and on?

A diagnosis, a meme

A small bird turns easily into a reaction meme,
while the Lone Tree in Carmel tries to laugh,
"How strange to be called lonely
when millions of people visit every year."

It's cold enough to sunburn and not notice,
the hot breath of skin blisters slowly—
I climb down to the water's edge
just to feel the edge of time,
and it's softer than I imagined.

What is stolen from me leaves pieces of stars
glittering in the yellow light and tar fields—
some words, a few electrical sparks, everything
and nothing much.
Please don't bleed picking up the pieces.

Blood is a betrayal. Clots wait
in the shadows. How surreal to know
how I will die but not when.
I turned a bird into a meme.

Skeleton of a fever of stingrays

A thornback's wing-like fins
with delicate splinters like soft bone,
formed and calcified like an exploding star
or a splitting embryo in those
first beats of life, cells dividing.

These bones are not bones,
the bone room card says~
*"It is all flexible cartilage
that holds their hatching eggs inside them,"*
holds them close until babies emerge whole.

The ampullae of Lorensinos pulse,
they hunt for food, mostly small creatures.
A fever of rays never stops moving—
their venomous spines pointing home
and some carry lightening in their hearts,
discharge their bolts to stunning display.

This Jurassic wife is stunning in formal wear
even when washed up, homeless,
drifting with jetsam, near Ocean Boulevard.
An exploding star with sharp electric wit—
Honeycomb Whiptail ray, Ribbon-tailed ray,
Blue Dotted ray, a parade of stunning beauties.
A fever of rays.

Cancer: Daily Horoscope for Summer Solstice

The moon is in Cancer. Retrograde.
The water is always cold. The sand is glass.
I trace the word, *stouthearted*, but it washes away.

The riptide took a man today. You will find love.
I stood there yesterday, felt the muscle and teeth of water.
I still have bite marks.

The moon is in Cancer. Your lucky numbers are 23, 32, and 7.
June is called the honeymoon because of bees and atmospheric dust.
I was once a beekeeper.

A bride is near the water. Venus reaches its direct station today.
Her dress is stained and dirty at the hem, smells like fish and salt.
She doesn't see the great white, migrating to warmer water.

The taste of honey is on my skin.
Sea salt, oil slicked water, and bird feathers cling to my legs.
The salt dries in cracked lines.

The stars are falling.

There be monsters here, too.

Calculation: Waiting for Gödel
(Incompleteness Theory)

Yesterday morning had gold in its mouth,
a joy known only between skin and tongue.
A mockingbird called out my name, called out
a word slipped through silvered beak and sun—

Blue. The completeness I feel when you
are here with me, flesh pressed against time,
which does not exist. And so I cut through
to count our iambic rhythm and rhyme.

When I am with you, time does not exist.
I try mathematically modeling birdsong;
why do my honey-speckled doubts persist?
Did fractal calculation get it wrong?

Syntactically incomplete by design,
such logics go; omission is the paradigm.

In Appreciation

Thank you for everyone that helped, that comforted my broken heart, listened to the poems while I rocked them to sleep, and kept the light on: Lenore Hart, Juliana Gray, Issa Lewis, Holly Peterson, Jessica Temple, Jennifer Givhan, Julie Weiss, and Katie Manning. I know I am forgetting more. Please forgive my flood-soaked hurricane fuzzied brain if you are not in this list, you are in my heart, always.

Special acknowledgment to Yun Wang, a Senior Research Scientist at Caltech who helped me fact check the abecedarian, *Astrophysics of Victimology*, and worked back-and-forth tirelessly with various drafts until I finally understood the concepts in relation to how I wanted them to sound in the poetic form. This was the hardest poem I have ever written.

A special thank you to James Reagan, who connected me with people in Prague that are both fans of the sonnet and very knowledgeable in Gödel's physics.

Thank you to the editor at *Mud Season Review*, Jonah Meyer, who accepted five science poems at once and reminded me that they still have a place in the world just as I was about to fold away this manuscript.

But most of all these are love poems. These are love poems that came out of a very strange landscape, one of desolation/fear/panic, and through the woods I walked and walked in my red coat to find friendship with the wolves and a home, finally. Thank you to the love and friendship that inspired all of it.

Danèlle Lejeune, poet and photographer

On Danèlle Lejeune's book tours, at coffee shops, at faculty parties, when folks find out that she was once a pig farmer in Iowa and now is a poet in Savannah, Georgia, they ask, wide-eyed and curious, "How on earth did she get here?" She often jokes that what happened involved a fourteen-foot American alligator, a strange Czech man in a bar in Minneapolis, and a pinch of Midwestern farm crisis. It's too long of a story for an author bio but will maybe someday be a Hallmark movie.

Danèlle's poetry conveys this grit, the loneliness of a decaying ecology of both earth and human spirit—but resilience too. Critics have said her ability to capture moments of tenderness are nothing short of image musicality. Her poetry bends these borders too, not quite a language poet of New York and not a Black Mountain Southerner either, she writes like a woman in a farm field with a broken heart, a goddess with bees swarming her like a halo, children sleeping at her feet.

You can find her work here at www.danellelejeune.com and at various galleries in the Southeast. You can find her arguing about onions and random historical trivia just outside Savannah, GA, in a brick house that has yet to blow down with her children and her husband novelist/poet Tony Morris. They run the Ossabaw Writers' Retreat together. They also have a cat that likes to trash-talk the neighbors, or everybody, really.

Danèlle's poems are physics and math-based, but don't let that scare you. Schrodinger's cat ends up in a domestic violence shelter, there's a love poem to the physicist who declared time doesn't exist, and we get to eavesdrop on bulldozers in couple's therapy. This book is an exploration of the landscape of math and science and poetry, where quantum entanglement explains true love, scientists drink morning tea while trying to explain fractals, the universe smells like raspberry dark chocolate, and Planck's constant measures what's left of a victim's dignity after leaving a dangerous homelife. Patterns build up, atoms explode, and we get to go home again, to something new and beautiful.